South Downs

David Hare was born in Sussex in 1947. He is the author
of twenty-eight plays for the stage, sixteen of which have
been seen at the National Theatre. These plays include
Plenty, *The Secret Rapture*, *Skylight*, *Amy's View*, *Via
Dolorosa*, *Stuff Happens*, *Gethsemane* and *The Power of
Yes*. In 1993 three plays about the Church, the Law and
the Labour Party – *Racing Demon*, *Murmuring Judges*
and *The Absence of War* – were presented in repertory in
the Olivier Theatre. His many screenplays for cinema and
television include *Licking Hitler*, *Damage*, *The Hours* and
The Reader. He directed his most recent television film,
Page Eight, for the BBC.

DAVID HARE

South Downs

with

Mere Fact, Mere Fiction

faber and faber

First published in 2011
by Faber and Faber Limited
74–77 Great Russell Street
London WC1B 3DA

Typeset by Country Setting, Kingsdown, Kent CT14 8ES
Printed and bound by CPI Group (UK) Ltd, Croydon CR0 4YY

A CIP record for this book
is available from the British Library

ISBN 978-0-571-27829-9

2 4 6 8 10 9 7 5 3 1

Author's Note

Terence Rattigan's play *The Browning Version*
is usually presented in a double bill with another
short play of his called *Harlequinade*.

In 2010 I was approached by the Rattigan estate
to write a new curtain-raiser for the hundredth
anniversary of Rattigan's birth.

My play is written as a tribute to Rattigan,
and aims to share common themes with his.

South Downs was first presented in a double bill with
Terence Rattigan's *The Browning Version* in the Minerva
Theatre at the Chichester Festival Theatre on 2 September
2011, with the following cast:

PUPILS

John Blakemore Alex Lawther
Jeremy Duffield Jonathan Bailey
Colin Jenkins Bradley Hall
Tommy Gunther Jack Elliott
Roger Sprule Liam Morton

MASTERS

Rev. Eric Dewley Nicholas Farrell
Basil Spear Andrew Woodall

PARENTS

Belinda Duffield Anna Chancellor
Sheila Blakemore Stella Gonet

Director Jeremy Herrin
Designer Tom Scutt
Lighting Designer Bruno Poet
Sound Designer Ian Dickinson
Music Paul Englishby

Characters

Pupils

John Blakemore
Jeremy Duffield
Colin Jenkins
Tommy Gunter
Roger Sprule

Masters

Rev. Eric Dewley
Basil Spear

Parents

Belinda Duffield
Sheila Blakemore
(voice only)

The play is set in a public school
in the South Downs in 1962.

The scenes are written to meld one into another,
without pause. Locations need not be defined.

SOUTH DOWNS

For Harper

'In a football match everything is complicated by the presence of the other team.'

Jean-Paul Sartre

ONE

First, four boys appear and sing the hymn 'Praise to the Lord, the Almighty, the King of Creation'. They go, then: Rev. Eric Dewley, an untidy man in his fifties, in flannels and dog collar, is welcoming a boy of fourteen to his study. John Blakemore, in regulation jacket, is an unsteady mix of confidence and insecurity.

Dewley Come in, please, Blakemore. Tell me what's bothering you.

Blakemore stands, saying nothing.

Blakemore. You requested to see me, can you please tell me what's bothering you?

Blakemore I can't, sir.

Dewley Why not?

Blakemore Because I thought there was something I could tell you, and now I realise I was wrong.

Dewley I see.

Blakemore You're a master.

Dewley waits, perplexed.

Dewley We're moving into paradox here, Blakemore. Do you know what a paradox is?

Blakemore Yes, sir.

Dewley The paradox is: you asked to see me. I didn't ask to see you. The original request came from you. Well? Am I right?

Blakemore You're right.

Dewley I was happy to agree. And now you refuse to talk to me. That's the paradox.

Blakemore is silent.

Presumably I am to know you're unhappy but I am not to know why.

Blakemore I never said I was unhappy.

Dewley So what's going on?

Blakemore I made a mistake, sir. I thought I could talk to you. And I can't.

TWO

Now Dewley is ushering a more senior boy, Jeremy Duffield, into the same study. Duffield has personalised his uniform with a waistcoat and fine jacket. He is seventeen and handsome, with lush black curls.

Dewley Ah, Duffield, good. Yes, I wanted to have a word with you. About the Debating Society.

Duffield Yes, sir.

Dewley I've been given the list of proposed subjects for next year's debates.

Duffield Yes.

Dewley It's an important principle that boys choose their own subjects.

Duffield Thank you, sir.

Dewley There's no question of you being made to debate things that don't interest you.

Dewley reads from a sheet of paper.

Monday January 21st, 'This house believes that the public schools should be abolished.' Monday January 28th, 'This house believes that the monarchy should be abolished.' Monday February 4th, 'This house believes that nuclear weapons should be abolished.' Really, Duffield, it appears that if you have your way there's going to be very little of this country left standing. Monday February 11th, 'This house believes that advertising is immoral and should be banned.' Monday February 18th, 'This house believes that the Church should be disestablished.' You don't think you're adopting a rather scorched-earth approach to the world's problems?

Duffield That's how people are feeling.

Dewley Really?

Duffield Yes, sir. In this part of Sussex.

Dewley looks at him doubtfully.

Dewley Well, Duffield, obviously you move in very different circles from me.

Duffield A lot of people are feeling we can't go on as we are.

Dewley But it's a real danger in life, I've seen it happen to boys before. I'm not lecturing you, Duffield. Please don't take me wrong.

Duffield I would never take you wrong.

Dewley At a certain age, young men become addicted to the idea of transformation. They long for everything to be different.

Duffield But isn't transformation at the heart of Our Lord's life, sir? He was utterly transformed.

Dewley He transformed us in our hearts, Duffield. About social questions He was much more guarded.

Duffield The trade-union chaplain who preached evensong last Sunday said Jesus came to earth to sweep everything away. After He came, everything was completely changed. We're living one life but very soon, He tells us, we'll be living another. It's a revolutionary message.

Dewley doesn't rise to this. He changes tactic.

Dewley Duffield, you remember I made you a prefect?

Duffield Certainly.

Dewley And, as your housemaster, when I made you a prefect I pointed out that we already had a full complement of prefects, we had quite enough prefects already. But to your considerable advantage it was within my discretion to make more. By making you a prefect, I was making a special point. I was, if you like, going out of my way.

Duffield My mother says that when Mr Wilson's elected we can all say goodbye to the public schools.

Dewley I've met your mother, haven't I?

Duffield Last term.

Dewley She – yes – memorably I've met her.

Duffield She came down.

Dewley Indeed.

Duffield To visit me. We all went to Brighton for roast lunch.

Dewley She's what?

Duffield She's an actress, sir. She's appearing at the Duke of York's in *Uncle Says No*.

Dewley Yes. That's right.

Duffield Well, it is right, yes.

Dewley And I agree with her about Mr Wilson.

Duffield She says we've seen nothing yet.

Dewley She's very likely correct.

Duffield And that's exactly why I've singled out these subjects. For debate. If we don't have the debate, then we're pretending these things aren't happening. You yourself say a school is part of society, it can't be separate from society. I've heard you insist on that so many times. We mustn't be cut off. I'm trying to make sure we're not.

Dewley is uncomfortable, unsure if he's being satirised.

Dewley And the other thing I'm concerned about, I'm speaking to you now in confidence, is Blakemore.

Duffield You're worried about Blakemore, sir?

Dewley I didn't say I was worried, I said I was concerned. He's well into his second year but has he settled?

Duffield Settled?

Dewley Has he found his level?

Duffield Has he been to see you, sir?

Dewley I don't know why you ask that.

Duffield I'm asking that.

Dewley And I'm asking why.

Duffield I couldn't help wondering if he'd been to see you, sir.

Dewley Did he say he'd seen me?

Duffield I'm asking you, sir.

Dewley Did he imply he'd been to see me?

Duffield I don't speak much to Blakemore, sir. Not unless I absolutely have to.

Dewley looks at him yet more mistrustfully.

Dewley Do you think you could possibly keep an eye on him and let me know if anything's amiss? Better still, why don't we strike a bargain? You look after Blakemore, and I'll allow this incendiary list of debates. Is that a deal?

THREE

A classroom. Blakemore is sitting next to a skinny, awkward boy of his own age called Colin Jenkins. The teacher in front of the class is Basil Spear, in his forties, short, pedantic, dangerous. He reads from a book in his hand.

Spear
'True wit is Nature to advantage dress'd,
What oft was thought, but ne'er so well express'd.'

Right, let's have a crack at this, shall we? Jenkins?

Jenkins I think, well, sir, I think what this might be is that he's saying everything's been said before.

Spear Everything's been said before?

Jenkins Yes. That's what he's trying to get at.

Spear looks at him a moment.

Spear Jenkins, let's start somewhere else, shall we?

Jenkins Sir.

Spear Let's clear our heads and begin again. Let's start by giving the poet some credit.

Jenkins Sir.

Spear Let's do the poet the honour of supposing he is not *trying* to say anything. Poets do not try to say anything. Most especially when they are of the stature of Alexander Pope.

Jenkins Yes, sir.

Spear We start by assuming that Pope has said exactly what he wants to say, and that unlike the rest of us, he's got beyond the trying stage.

Jenkins Yes, sir.

Spear Again, Jenkins.

Jenkins looks round a moment.

Jenkins I think what he's trying to get at is –

Spear Jenkins, hold steady, we don't seem to be making headway here. What is it I just said?

Jenkins Sir?

Spear What did I just say? About Pope? What did I just say?

Jenkins When?

Spear Just now.

Jenkins I don't know.

Spear Did you hear what I said?

Jenkins I never don't.

Spear is not backing down.

Spear Jenkins, I want you to listen to me.

Jenkins I'm listening.

Spear Alexander Pope is one of the greatest poets who ever lived. Take my word for that. He does not say something *like* what he wants to say, or something *near* what he wants to say, or even something approximate to what he wants to say. Never, Jenkins, does Pope splatter the target. When he says something, he says it and it stays said.

'True wit is nature to advantage dressed;
What oft was thought but ne'er so well expressed.'

Again.

Jenkins looks round again, desperate.

Jenkins Everything's been said.

Spear Yes?

Jenkins It's just how you put it.

Spear 'Everything's been said. It's just how you put it'?

Jenkins Yes.

Spear 'Everything's been said. It's just how you put it'?

Jenkins Yes.

Spear Is that your contemporary paraphrase?

Jenkins I think that's what he's trying to say.

Spear looks at him unkindly.

Spear When they handed out brains, Jenkins, it's clear you were at the back of the queue. Or were you entertaining yourself in some other queue altogether?

Jenkins does not answer.

Blakemore?

Blakemore In the eighteenth century everyone believed that certain truths were eternal. So the job was to re-state the familiar, only to do it more cleverly. You had to find new ways of dressing it up. Jenkins is right. He's basically right. Then in the nineteenth century, along came the Romantic movement, that's people like Wordsworth and Shelley, and they think there are plenty of new things to say. In fact they saw Pope as a bit of a throwback.

Spear A what?

Blakemore A throwback. They saw him as a spokesman for his class.

Spear Did they?

Blakemore I think they did.

Spear Go on.

Blakemore Because if you say the only wisdom is the existing wisdom, then if you think about it, that's actually what all the rich people want you to say. You're serving their interests. Because if you say 'There's nothing more to say, it's all been said,' what are you actually saying? Everything's as it should be. Which is what the rich always say. 'There's not much you can do about it, chum. That's how it is. Live with it.' And that's really what Pope's saying. That whole 'nature' thing of his, I think it's a cover, isn't it? Because nature to him isn't trees and bushes, it's nothing really changing. 'There it is,' Pope says. 'You can't beat nature.' No wonder he was so popular with the rich.

Spear looks at him a moment.

Spear You've obviously thought about this, Blakemore.

Blakemore I've given it some thought, yes.

Spear Clearly.

Blakemore But Jenkins has thought about it too.

Spear You think he has?

Blakemore Just as hard as me.

Spear Maybe, but Jenkins didn't express himself with quite the same authority, did he?

Blakemore He expressed himself in his own way. I knew what he meant. In fact I think you and I both knew what he meant. We both knew perfectly well.

Spear is bristling, detecting an enemy.

Spear You're walking a very fine line, Blakemore. There's a very fine line between precocity and insolence, and you just crossed it.

Blakemore I didn't intend to cross it, sir.

Spear Didn't you?

Blakemore I didn't cross it knowingly.

Spear Well that's a question of interpretation, isn't it? And in this classroom my interpretation is the one which prevails.

Spear looks a moment, then turns to the whole class.

What Pope is doing – and notice I say 'doing', Jenkins, not 'trying to do' – what Pope is doing is freeing poets from the burden of originality. There is no obligation to be original, only an obligation to be memorable. Free verse, said Robert Frost, is like playing tennis with the net down. Pope puts the net up. And he puts it high. As high as it can go. Express yourself, yes, by all means, but express yourself better than anyone has ever expressed themselves before. The chances are that none of us in this room – not you, Jenkins, not you, Blakemore, not even I – will come up with a single original thought in the whole of our long lives. Because everything we can possibly think has already been thought by somebody somewhere before. There is no such thing as originality. But far from depressing us, that prospect, on the contrary, should set us free. It should reassure us. Dreary modern poets pour forth drivel with no rules. Pope gives us rigid rules. But the lesson of poetry, as much as the lesson of life, is that only within a cage do we find freedom.

The school bell rings.

Monday!

FOUR

Jenkins and Blakemore are on their stencilled tuck boxes, each with half a pint of bottled milk and sharing a cigarette.

Blakemore My father's away. He's always away.

Jenkins Where is he?

Blakemore He's at sea.

Jenkins Why?

Blakemore Because that's his job. He's a sailor.

Jenkins Oh, so that's his reason.

Blakemore Yes.

Jenkins Does he ever write?

Blakemore He writes to my mother. On blue flimsies.

Jenkins But does he write to you?

Blakemore We only see him for three weeks a year. He goes to Australia, and then comes home. And every time he comes home Mum cries.

Jenkins Why does she cry?

Blakemore Because she hasn't seen him for so long.

Jenkins That doesn't make sense.

Blakemore Why not?

Jenkins Because if she never sees him, and then she does, then surely she should be happy?

Blakemore ignores this question. Jenkins passes the shared butt.

Blakemore He has a big roll.

Jenkins Big roll of what?

Blakemore A big roll of money. With an elastic band. He keeps it in his inside pocket, so it comes out warm. When he's back from a voyage, he takes out his roll. We go for a steak on the seafront in Hastings. We get steak every time Dad comes home. With fried mushrooms. It's incredible – when he pays, he unpeels a note from his roll.

Jenkins is cutting pieces of a chocolate cake from his tuck box.

Jenkins Do you want some cake?

Blakemore I don't eat cake.

Jenkins I get sent one every week, so there's plenty.

Jenkins eats and smokes at the same time.

Is that why you're here then?

Blakemore Where?

Jenkins Here. Did they send you to school because your mother can't cope?

Blakemore No.

Jenkins Why are you here then? Why did they send you here?

Blakemore Same reason as everyone else, I suppose.

Jenkins You're not like everyone else.

Blakemore Yes I am.

Jenkins You're not.

Blakemore blushes.

Don't pretend you are, because you're not. You're different.

Blakemore I was meant to go to Winchester but I got scarlet fever. I couldn't leave home to take the exam, because I was highly contagious.

Jenkins You could have done the exam in your bedroom.

Blakemore No.

Jenkins You could.

Blakemore No, I couldn't.

Jenkins You could.

Blakemore We asked to do that, and they said it wasn't allowed.

Jenkins They could easily have slipped the papers under the door.

Blakemore You've never had scarlet fever. For a start, everything you touch is infected. Literally, everything. If I touched a book, they burnt it. They burnt the sheets from my bed. I had a boiled egg and I sicked it straight back up.

Jenkins I think if Winchester had really wanted to take you, they would have found a way.

Blakemore It's not as easy as that.

Jenkins Why not?

Blakemore Because I had to get a scholarship.

Jenkins Why?

Blakemore I couldn't go without a scholarship.

Jenkins Why not?

Blakemore Because.

Jenkins Because what?

Blakemore Just because.

Jenkins Why didn't your dad get out his roll?

Blakemore doesn't answer.

Well? Couldn't he have peeled some fivers off his famous roll?

Blakemore is lost for a moment, then gets up.

Blakemore I've got to go, I've got piano. I hate Thursdays, English with Basil Queer, then piano with Raging Queer.

Jenkins Is the piano man queer?

Blakemore All piano men are queer. You know that.

Jenkins I don't.

Blakemore He spills ash on my knee while I'm playing.

Jenkins I don't do piano.

Blakemore He comes specially from Worthing. Why would you do that if you weren't queer?

Jenkins I'm not taking up piano. Whatever happens.

Blakemore All teachers are queer. That's why they're teachers. Because they get to spend the whole day with us. And that's what they want. What do you think they're all doing at the swimming pool? Watching us. Because we're not allowed to wear swimming trunks.

Jenkins There's a reason for that.

Blakemore Oh, is there?

Jenkins There's a good reason. You've heard them. You've heard what they say.

Blakemore I've heard them.

Jenkins They say if we wore swimming trunks, the fibres would block up the filters. The filters would be clogged.

Blakemore And you believe them? Is that why they're all watching? To check the filters don't get clogged?

Jenkins That's what they say.

Blakemore Believe that, you believe anything.

Jenkins I'm telling you what they say.

Jenkins has stubbed out his cigarette and closed his tuck box.

Why did your father go to sea?

Blakemore I don't know.

Jenkins Don't you know why he went?

Blakemore It's not like he's just started going. He always did. His whole life. He ran away from school to be a sailor. He started as a cornet.

Jenkins A cornet?

Blakemore Yes.

Jenkins Bollocks. A cornet's an ice-cream.

Blakemore The cornet blows reveille. He's the most junior person on the ship. My dad joined the navy as a cornet.

Jenkins Yeah.

Blakemore What does 'yeah' mean?

Jenkins Yeah.

Blakemore You keep saying 'yeah'.

Jenkins Yeah. I know why he went.

Blakemore Why do you think he went?

Jenkins It's obvious. To get away from you. And your so-called 'mum', I expect.

Jenkins goes. Blakemore stands a moment.

FIVE

Blakemore is skulking along a corridor. Duffield, splendid, stops him.

Duffield Blakemore, come here. Can I ask you a question?

Blakemore You can ask me anything you like.

Duffield It's the obvious question. What the fuck were you doing?

Blakemore I wasn't doing anything.

Duffield What the fuck were you up to? Are you out of your fucking mind? Did you go and speak to Eric the Hysteric?

Blakemore No.

Duffield Why did you do that? Why did you speak to him?

Blakemore I didn't speak to him.

Duffield You went to see him. It's an objective historical fact, based on observable data. What did you go to say?

Blakemore I didn't say anything.

Duffield You did.

Blakemore No. I asked to see him, but when I got there I didn't say anything. I didn't. I promise, I didn't.

Duffield When you got there, you didn't say anything. And is that normal behaviour? Is that how normal people behave?

Blakemore can't answer. Duffield glances up and down the corridor, making sure they're alone.

Do you have a revolver under your pillow?

Blakemore I don't. No.

Duffield You know Bannister had to be taken away.

Blakemore I heard rumours, I didn't know if they were true.

Duffield They're true.

Blakemore Nobody was meant to know, were we?

Duffield Well, no, you weren't. Because they found a revolver under his pillow.

Blakemore He disappeared very suddenly.

Duffield He certainly did.

Blakemore He was with us for Latin. He was a year behind because he was useless at Latin. He couldn't parse.

Duffield Bannister said he had a revolver for shooting crows, that's what he said. But it wasn't Bannister that got blamed, was it?

Blakemore doesn't answer, not knowing what he is meant to say.

Do you understand nothing? Do you understand what I'm saying?

Blakemore You're going to have to help me a little.

Duffield Are you one of those very clever people who understands what no one else understands, but then doesn't understand what everyone else understands?

Blakemore I think I may be, yes. Because I have no idea what you're getting at, Duffield.

Blakemore's sincerity is a touch desperate. Duffield waits, then explains.

Duffield Bannister was going to shoot himself. My point is that nobody blamed Bannister. The person who got blamed was his prefect. Why? Because the prefect wasn't psychic, that's why.

Blakemore Oh, I get it now.

Duffield His prefect didn't guess what lay below Bannister's pillow. And that's what happens. That's the basic injustice. Blakemore, if you decide to kill yourself, it isn't you that gets blamed. It's me.

Blakemore I must say, that doesn't seem fair.

Duffield It's not fair at all, because at any point crackpots can bring good men down.

Duffield looks again, softening.

Look, I'm going to be honest with you. Tommy Gunter is saying you're in love with Jenkins.

Blakemore I'm not in love with Jenkins. Why does he say that? That's crazy.

Duffield I don't mind if you're in love with Jenkins, it's your business as far as I'm concerned. But Gunter saw you sharing the same cigarette, which apart from anything is downright unhygienic. And if you want a cigarette, you're meant to hide.

Blakemore We did hide. We locked the door.

Duffield You walk a mile into the woods and then have a cigarette.

Blakemore Aren't people allowed to have friends? What are you saying? Other people have friends. Why can't I?

Duffield So you're not denying it?

Blakemore Of course I'm denying it.

Duffield If you love someone, you don't betray them, Blakemore. Not in public. You don't deny them.

Blakemore I don't love Jenkins!

Duffield shrugs slightly.

I don't love Jenkins!

Duffield Is that what's unhinging you?

Blakemore Nothing's unhinging me.

Duffield Something's making you unhappy.

Blakemore looks at him, resentful.

Apparently something weird happened in Basil Queer's class.

Blakemore Nothing happened.

Duffield That's not what I've been told.

Blakemore, perhaps fearing tears, is defiant.

Blakemore Tell me then. If it's all so bloody shocking and wrong. Why can't you tell me?

Duffield You rode to Jenkins' defence on some obscure literary point. Everyone noticed. There was no one in that class who didn't notice what was going on.

Blakemore What did they notice?

Duffield You stuck your neck out. Like some medieval knight rescuing a maiden.

Blakemore It wasn't like that. Who said it was like that?

Duffield You scooped Jenkins up and rode off on your steed.

Blakemore Basil Queer was being impossible.

Duffield Basil Queer is a jerk, everyone knows that.

Duffield shakes his head at the irony of it.

The funny thing is I actually like you, Blakemore. I do. But then I have a weakness for effeminates.

Blakemore Because your mother's an actress.

Duffield Yeah. She is actually. How do you know that?

Blakemore Because I've seen her on the stage.

Duffield In person?

Blakemore Well of course in person, she was on the stage.

Duffield How old *are* you, Blakemore? You claim to be fourteen. Something tells me you're actually twenty-three and faking.

Blakemore Because I get a cheap day return to go to the West End.

Duffield Not from here you don't.

Blakemore No. From home. I go from home.

Duffield Your mother lets you go? She lets you go alone to London?

Duffield is genuinely surprised. Blakemore feels he may be winning at last.

Blakemore And I'm not effeminate.

Duffield No, but you know what it means. You're fourteen and you know what 'effeminate' means. That doesn't speak well for you, Blakemore. Luckily I'm not shocked. I don't shock easily. If you have a mother on the stage you know everyone's acting anyway.

Blakemore is in danger of being overwhelmed by Duffield's unexpected kindness.

Please don't cry, it demeans you.

Blakemore is holding on. When he speaks he is quiet, reasonable.

Blakemore I don't understand why I can't be friends with Jenkins. You have friends. You've got countless friends. You're about the most popular person in the school. You throw away more friends than I ever make. You even go into town with Siegfried. So why can't I be friends with Jenkins?

Duffield You know perfectly well.

Blakemore Can I tell you what's odd? I don't.

Duffield is thoughtful.

Duffield All right. All right, I'll spell it out. If you really want to know. It's deviation from the norm.

Blakemore Can someone explain to me what the norm is?

Duffield Everyone knows what the norm is.

Blakemore Well, I don't.

Duffield There are friends and friends, Blakemore.

Duffield lets this thought stand a moment.

And please don't go and bother Eric the Hysteric again. If you have a problem, cut out the middle man, come straight to me.

Blakemore I don't have a problem.

Duffield You've got 'problem' written all over you.

Blakemore What happened to Bannister?

Duffield I don't know. They took him away. To a mental ward.

Duffield stops. His warning stands.

Blakemore, I was like you. I was. For a long time, I was like you. Then I learnt the rules.

SIX

Dewley is addressing four boys: Blakemore, Jenkins, Tommy Gunter, and Roger Sprule. Gunter is fifteen, dishevelled and dirty, Sprule is also fifteen, dark-haired, post-pubescent, strong. All four are in pyjamas and dressing gowns.

Dewley You are used to thinking of me as a teacher. But this evening I want you to think of me as a fellow human being. All right, everyone?

All Yes, sir.

Dewley Mrs Dewley will bring biscuits at the end of our session.

He waits as they absorb this information.

So. You are to become full members of the Anglican communion. To claim membership, you must first learn the significance of the Eucharist.

Gunter What's the Eucharist?

Dewley The Eucharist is the act of Holy Communion.

Gunter Is it when we drink the wine, sir?

Dewley It is. It is that moment.

Dewley looks at him, wary.

The service of Holy Communion is the recreation of the meal at which Jesus offered bread and wine to His disciples on the night before His death. When we eat the bread and drink the wine, we receive Christ whole and entire. At that moment, He is what we call 'a real presence'. I don't see how there can be any more important moment in any young person's life.

Gunter is staring at him, wanting to speak.

Dewley Gunter?

Gunter I agree, sir.

Dewley Good. That's a good attitude with which to be going into this.

Blakemore has put up his hand.

Blakemore?

Blakemore I've got a question.

Dewley There's no need to raise your hand.

Blakemore When you eat the wafer, perhaps I've got this wrong, but is the idea that it's Christ's body?

Dewley That is also a very good question. A very interesting question.

Blakemore And is the idea that you're actually drinking His blood?

Dewley The best way I can answer is to tell you that opinions are divided.

Blakemore People don't agree?

Dewley That's right.

Blakemore There are different views?

Dewley About what's happening at the sacred moment itself.

Blakemore It's just that earlier you did say we were eating the body of Christ.

Dewley No, to be fair to myself, I said no such thing. I very specifically did not say that. In fact I always go out of my way, when preparing boys, not to use divisive language.

Blakemore No, but some people do say that, don't they?

Dewley They do. Yes.

Blakemore Catholics.

Dewley That's right. You're right, Blakemore. This is what Catholics believe.

Blakemore I thought so.

Dewley Or particularly what Roman Catholics believe. At the moment the bread is eaten, it becomes the body. At the moment the wine is drunk, it becomes the blood.

There is a short silence, as everyone takes this in.

For a Roman Catholic, this is not a question of perception. It's not a matter of how they see it. It's a matter of material change. It's a miracle and it's a mystery.

Blakemore And what do we believe?

Dewley Well, interesting, again. Within the Anglican Church you find many points of view. In fact, you find all points of view.

Blakemore Yes, but what I'm asking is, what's yours?

Gunter stirs, annoyed.

Gunter He's about to tell you, if you give him a chance.

Dewley Thank you, but Blakemore's question is a fair one, Gunter.

Gunter He's always like this.

Dewley Gunter.

Gunter He shows off.

Dewley Gunter.

Gunter He shows off in biology.

Dewley Can I make a distinction here, please?

Gunter Because he always wants to prove how clever he is.

Dewley This is not a lesson, Gunter. What did I say at the beginning?

Blakemore Exactly.

Dewley This is not an exam for which you are sitting. Blakemore is proceeding in a spirit of genuine inquiry, and that is a spirit I wish to encourage. This is a chance to ask questions.

Dewley waits.

Gunter?

Gunter Nothing.

Dewley Nothing what?

Gunter Nothing to ask.

Dewley I have the feeling you're sulking.

Gunter I'm not sulking.

Dewley It's very important, Gunter, during this process to put personal feelings aside. It would be very sad if you missed your chance to grasp the principles of Anglicanism simply because you dislike Blakemore.

Gunter says nothing. Dewley resumes.

To explain. Soon after the Anglican Church was founded by Henry the Eighth, Elizabeth the First gave her assent to the Thirty-Nine Articles.

Sprule suddenly erupts into life.

Sprule Transubstantiation.

Dewley Sprule?

Sprule That's what it's called.

Dewley Absolutely correct.

Sprule It's called transubstantiation.

Dewley Good. The belief that Christ becomes the offering is indeed called transubstantiation.

Sprule I've heard people talk about it.

Dewley Roman Catholics believe Christ dies every day, and so every day priests perform a mass to reenact His death. Protestants believe He died only once. As Anglicans therefore we prefer not to speak of transubstantiation. We tend to speak of consubstantiation. The bread is 'as if' it is Christ's body. The wine is 'as if' it is Christ's blood. Elizabeth's advisers saw no scriptural justification for what they viewed as a barbaric act. Christ is your best friend. Why would you eat and drink your best friend?

The group is frowning now, cowed.

Blakemore?

Blakemore I'm having trouble with this, sir.

Dewley What troubles you?

Blakemore It seems odd.

Dewley Odd in what way?

He throws a side glance at Gunter, who is shifting.

Gunter, please allow Blakemore to ask his question. Blakemore?

Blakemore We're Anglo-Catholics, is that right?

Dewley You're at an Anglo-Catholic school.

Blakemore We're High Church.

Dewley That's one way of putting it.

Sprule Smells and bells.

Dewley smiles, tacit.

Blakemore All right, I get it, I can see what other people believe.

Dewley Good.

Blakemore But I'm still asking: what do we believe?

Gunter He just told you. He just told you what we believe.

Dewley Gunter.

Gunter It's impossible! It's impossible to have a class with him.

Dewley That isn't true, Gunter.

Gunter Excuse me, sir, but you explained it perfectly clearly. 'We don't believe in transubstantiation, we believe in consubstantiation.' What could be clearer than that?

Dewley That isn't exactly what I said.

Gunter And yet still he goes on! Why do I have to do confirmation with him? We're going to be here till

midnight, I've missed *Hancock's Half Hour*, and all so
that Blakemore can act like a pseud.

> *Dewley is in pain. There is a helpless silence. Gunter*
> *mutters.*

And what does it matter?

Dewley I'm sorry?

Gunter What does it matter anyway? We all have to
believe something because five hundred years ago Henry
the Eighth wanted a divorce?

> *Another miserable silence. Dewley turns to Blakemore.*

Dewley Blakemore?

Blakemore Yes.

Dewley You asked a question?

Blakemore Yes.

Dewley Please repeat it.

Blakemore Yes, sir. I asked what we believed.

> *Dewley considers, then speaks calmly, kindly.*

Dewley We believe in ritual and in rite, and in the wisdom
of tradition. We do things for the simple and excellent
reason that they have been done before. As our critics
allege, there is an element of theatre, yes. We admit that.
But we find comfort in theatre. We most certainly do not
share all points of doctrine with Rome. But we do see
ourselves as part of a Catholic tradition. We believe in
confession and in forgiveness. We look for the outward
and visible signs of an inward and invisible grace.

Blakemore Do we believe in sin?

Dewley Yes. We believe in sin.

There is a silence.

You're looking unhappy, Gunter.

Gunter No.

Dewley Does sin bother you?

Gunter doesn't answer.

Some time before the war I went to the Old Vic. I saw one of Shakespeare's plays. I don't know the name of the actor, it wasn't important who it was. A man called Prospero was master of an island. At a certain moment he had to reach out to his slave. He said some words. I knew the moment he said them, I'd never forget them. 'This thing of darkness I acknowledge mine.' It was the most Christian thing I'd ever heard. Because he wasn't really talking about the slave. He was talking about himself.

The group is silent now, Dewley is absorbed in his own thoughts. He looks up.

The dark is inside us, Gunter. If you don't feel that, you feel nothing. I can't teach that.

SEVEN

Blakemore and Jenkins are sitting in the boot-room, still in their pyjamas and dressing gowns, talking quietly.

Jenkins What do you want from me?

Blakemore I don't want anything.

Jenkins Yes, you do. And it's not even to touch my tool.

Blakemore I've seen your tool. I certainly don't want to touch it.

Jenkins Something more than that.

Blakemore What then?

Jenkins You've got a funny idea of friendship, Blakemore. You want something I can't give. It's tiring.

Silence. An impasse.

Blakemore No, I don't.

Jenkins It's tiring being with you. Because, for a start, you want to be with me all the time.

Blakemore No, I don't.

Jenkins And all the time you're with me, you want something from me.

Blakemore I get all I need.

Jenkins Some response. You drain the life out of people.

Another difficult moment.

Besides which, I like seeing other friends. Wadham has credit at the tuck shop. His family put ten pounds down at the beginning of term.

Blakemore He's buying your friendship. He's buying you like a tart.

Jenkins And you're not?

Blakemore How can I buy anything? I haven't told anyone, don't tell anyone, but we live in a semi-detached.

Jenkins I know. Everyone knows that already. You can't keep that sort of thing secret round here.

Jenkins is irritated.

Oh, don't look so sorry for yourself. You'll be all right, Blakemore. You'll do well in life. But whatever it is, it won't be worth doing.

Blakemore looks even more hurt, but Jenkins doesn't notice.

What did it mean?

Blakemore When?

Jenkins When Eric said he had the darkness inside him? What the fuck did that mean?

Blakemore I liked him when he said that. It's the first time I've liked him.

Jenkins It was spooky.

Blakemore I didn't think so.

Jenkins What was he saying? 'This thing of darkness.' What thing of darkness? Was he saying he was queer?

Blakemore No. No, of course not.

Jenkins I thought, 'Hang on, here we go, what's happening here?'

Blakemore No, it wasn't that.

Jenkins Wasn't it?

Blakemore No. Not at all.

Jenkins What then?

Blakemore You know what Eric's like. He had a bad war.

Jenkins Oh yeah.

Blakemore Well, he did. His best friend was eviscerated.

Jenkins Oh sure.

Blakemore It's true. His best friend died in Eric's arms.

Jenkins They all say that. They all say they had a bad war. Basil Queer says he strangled a German with his bare hands. And we're meant to believe that's why he's such a shit.

Jenkins gets up, discontented.

And you've started this thing of pretending to care about things you can't do anything about.

Blakemore What kind of things?

Jenkins Nuclear bombs. The end of the world.

Blakemore Those.

Jenkins That makes you grown-up, does it? I don't think so. Care about things which actually concern you.

Blakemore The world concerns me.

Jenkins Oh, give us a break! In English when you started talking about Sartre, a couple of boys had to go out and vomit in the quad. What does it look like for me? It makes me look stupid. I'm best friends with someone nobody likes.

Blakemore I don't like me either. But it's the character I've been given, and I can't do anything about it.

Jenkins Why can't you shut up? That's the obvious. That's the first step. Say less. It's not so hard. It's what I do.

But Blakemore is riled by this.

Blakemore So all right then, if that's what you do, Jenkins, come on, at confirmation, you were there, did you understand it?

Jenkins What?

Blakemore Transubstantiation!

Jenkins Of course not. It's a mystery. You're not *meant* to understand it. That's what a mystery is. It's something you don't understand. Why can't you leave it at that?

34

Nobody in the history of the world has ever understood transubstantiation, and Blakemore will?

Jenkins shakes his head at the absurdity.

Gunter said even Duffield gave you a bollocking.

Blakemore He didn't give me a bollocking.

Jenkins That's what Gunter said.

Blakemore And do you believe anything Gunter says?

Jenkins Why else would Duffield bother to talk to you?

Blakemore Because he was . . . sorting out a misunderstanding.

Jenkins Duffield's all right.

Blakemore He's more than all right. If I could come back a second time, I'd come back as Duffield. I admire Duffield beyond words.

Jenkins Why?

Blakemore Because he knows everything. Girls are going to love him.

Jenkins They love him already from what I've heard.

Blakemore He says something, people accept it. When I say the same thing, they say 'What a prat!'

Jenkins That's age.

Blakemore No. It's command. I don't have it. He has.

Jenkins looks, weakening a moment.

Jenkins You know what's going to happen?

Blakemore No.

Jenkins You know what I have to do. I have to see less of you. I have to be my own man.

Blakemore If you have to.

Jenkins We have to put distance between us. We're at that point.

Blakemore says nothing.

I can't do Saint's Day.

Blakemore OK.

Jenkins I can't do it.

Blakemore OK.

Jenkins I've promised Theodosius I'll go cycling with him.

Blakemore Well, that'll be a bundle of laughs.

Jenkins What will you do?

Blakemore When?

Jenkins On Saint's Day?

Blakemore looks at him a moment.

Blakemore Oh, don't worry about me.

EIGHT

Blakemore is sitting in the house study by himself, reading. Duffield comes in, out of school uniform, casually dressed.

Duffield We're wondering what you're doing.

Blakemore Duffield.

Duffield It's a beautiful autumn day. My mother and I were wondering what you were doing.

Blakemore I'm reading.

Duffield On a Saint's Day?

Blakemore Yes.

Duffield What are you reading on a Saint's Day?

Blakemore *L'Etranger* by Camus.

Duffield Is that a good book?

Blakemore It's about a man who ought to feel things, but doesn't.

Duffield And do you like it? Do you like the book?

Blakemore doesn't answer for a moment.

Blakemore?

Blakemore Duffield, please go away.

He has spoken in a small, sad voice. Duffield looks at him, thoughtful.

The whole school is empty, there's no one here, everyone's in Brighton. It's a holiday. Why pick on me?

Duffield Well, only that my mother wants to ask you to tea.

Blakemore I don't think that's very likely.

Duffield She's asking you.

Blakemore Now?

Duffield Does now not suit you?

From offstage, the sound of a woman's voice.

Belinda (*off*) Where is he, Jeremy? Where's my admirer?

Blakemore looks at Duffield, unforgiving.

Blakemore If this is a joke, I'll kill you.

Duffield It's not a joke. Belinda Duffield's asking you to tea.

NINE

*Duffield's study. Belinda Duffield is pouring tea for
Blakemore and Duffield. She is dark, gamine, barely
forty, and oddly summery, in a full-pleated skirt and tiny
jumper. There is a luxurious fruit cake, and good china.*

Belinda Do you eat cake?

Blakemore I don't normally, no.

Belinda Not normally?

Blakemore I don't eat it.

Belinda But will you make an exception for me? I never
met a man who didn't secretly like cake.

Blakemore I'm not yet a man.

Belinda This is from Fortnum and Mason. Which, if you
liked cake, would impress you. Or maybe it wouldn't.
You don't look like you're easily impressed.

Blakemore blushes.

Jeremy says you've been in trouble. That's good. I like a
rebel. It was you, wasn't it?

Blakemore Yes. I wrote the letter to the *Daily Express*.

Belinda I never saw it. What did it say?

Blakemore It said that at this school everyone's allowed
to wear a religious badge, like a crucifix, say, or Scripture
Union, but I wasn't allowed to wear my CND badge.

Belinda Aren't you?

Blakemore No.

Belinda Funny, Jeremy wears his all the time.

Duffield In the holidays, Mother. Not at school.

Duffield smiles tolerantly at Belinda.

Blakemore The Hysteric sent for me.

Belinda And what did he say?

Blakemore He said it was a rule. I said it was a silly rule. He said that's not the point.

Belinda What is the point?

Blakemore Obedience.

Belinda Ah.

Blakemore After all, he said, most rules are silly. But they're rules, and if we don't obey them we're savages.

Belinda Gosh.

Blakemore He said if I wanted, I could set fire to the corn in the North Field and burn the whole school down. It was as easy as that.

Belinda So that was his argument? By writing a letter you were endangering the survival of the school?

Blakemore Sort of. Yes.

Belinda Interesting.

Blakemore He said civilisation operates by consent. At any point any one of us can destroy any other. It's the exercise of self-restraint which makes society possible.

Belinda And what did you say?

Blakemore I said it had never occurred to me the school was weak. To me, it felt strong. In fact, very strong. It was hardly likely to be destroyed by a letter to the *Daily Express*.

Belinda No. But I suppose the letter came as a surprise. To the school, I mean.

Blakemore I signed it 'A pupil'.

Belinda Did you?

Blakemore But Tommy Gunter doesn't like me, so he went to Eric and told them 'A pupil' was me.

Belinda Yes. Probably it would have been wiser to have given them some warning.

Blakemore I was going to. I set off to see Eric.

Duffield This is the real problem, I think.

Belinda Why? Why is it the real problem?

There is a silence. A difficult confession.

Blakemore Because when I got there, I realised Eric wasn't someone I could talk to.

Belinda Really? Who can you talk to?

Belinda waits. Blakemore is on the verge of tears.

Jeremy, can't you go and play squash or something?

Duffield I'll go out for a cigarette.

Belinda Have at least two.

Duffield goes out.

That's better, isn't it? Fifty per cent less male in the room. More tea?

Blakemore Yes, please.

Belinda Do nuclear weapons really worry you, or are you just unhappy at school? John?

Blakemore can't answer.

It's a difficult question, isn't it? I don't like the idea of being burnt to a crisp either, but if I wrote a protest letter to the paper they'd say, 'Oh she's a stupid actress,' or,

'She's trying to publicise her play.' And it's true, our play isn't doing terribly well.

Blakemore It was full when I saw it.

Belinda You're very kind. It's a strange thing, you see, people are always more interested in motive than they are in what you're actually saying.

Blakemore I think it's wrong I can't wear my badge. It's wrong. It's a limitation on freedom.

Belinda Yes.

Belinda waits a moment.

Is this a very bad time for you?

Blakemore It's not an easy time. I lost my faith.

Belinda Goodness.

Belinda smiles, then instantly apologises.

I'm sorry, I didn't mean to sound glib.

Blakemore It's all right.

Belinda No, really. How did that happen?

Blakemore We went to confirmation class and it all seemed such nonsense. Having to stand up in public in front of hundreds of people and say you're a Christian. Surely if you really do think Christ's your saviour, it's private, isn't it? Isn't it a private thing?

Belinda I wonder, forgive me for asking this, but have you thought about dissembling?

Blakemore I don't know what dissembling means.

Belinda It's what most of us do. Most of the time.

Blakemore What is it?

Belinda Another way of saying it: have you thought about acting? Oh, I don't mean professionally, I mean in life.

Blakemore I haven't, no.

Belinda It's odd, women find acting easier than men. Pretending to be someone else doesn't threaten us. We're used to the idea of negotiation. Men want things from us, we have to deny them and not hurt their feelings. It's a skill. Generally, life's unendurable till you meet the opposite sex. Mine was, anyway. The only problem is, most men are terrified of women. It's a shame, it's boring for them and it's boring for us. Are you terrified?

Blakemore I don't know any women. Except my sister and my mother. And they don't count.

They smile. Blakemore is relaxing now.

Belinda What's your mother like?

Blakemore Scottish. She believes in education. She thinks education's the way out.

Belinda Really? The way out of what?

Blakemore Mum showed me the Marks and Spencer's annual report. She said, 'Look at the board, all of them are accountants.'

Belinda She wants you to be an accountant? That'll be marvellous. You can be my accountant. God knows, I need one. You like Jeremy?

Blakemore Very much.

Belinda Everyone does. He has his father's charm. I've told him charm is a terrible trap. Because it makes you lazy. You should be thankful you don't have it.

Blakemore Do I not have it at all?

Belinda Not a trace. You have something else.

Blakemore Did Jeremy ask you to speak to me?

Belinda smiles, conceding.

Belinda Jeremy's got Eric twisted round his little finger. So I know for a fact he went and petitioned on your behalf.

Blakemore He did? He didn't tell me.

Belinda He said writing a letter's hardly a sacking offence.

Blakemore Mum was furious.

Belinda Well, she would be.

Blakemore She thinks the most important thing in life is not to get noticed. On no account draw attention to yourself.

Belinda smiles again.

Belinda Johnny Gielgud says after fifty performances you always go stale. He says no one can keep it fresh for more than fifty. But I've done many more. I've done forty years. You don't have a cigarette, do you?

Blakemore No.

Blakemore frowns, not understanding her.

Belinda You're right. It's a funny time, isn't it? They built these places for a reason and now the reason's gone. Empire! So we all become curators of what people used to believe. Mr Wilson says that when the technology arrives everything's going to change. The thing I'm hoping for is a personal power pack. You know, put it on your back and then fly to the shops. But Mr Wilson also says they'll only invest in things for which there's a commercial imperative. And my flying to Harrods probably isn't top of their list. I don't know how much will really change, do you? In films they always show the future being white, I don't know why. Everyone walking around in white clothes. You think, why would people give up the pleasure of colour? When I think of my own life . . . Jamie

43

proposed to me at dinner at the Savoy in 1942, and I'll never forget the ruby red of the Château Haut-Brion against the white tablecloth. Would it really be progress to lose colour? Lurid colour. It was much the best wine I'd ever drunk.

Blakemore He seduced you?

Belinda stares, serious, but doesn't answer.

Belinda Jamie went off to the desert and was killed. A bullet in the throat. Which in a way is easier. He never saw Jeremy. So at least it was clear. Whereas I gather your father is half there and half not, which is trickier. People should either be alive or dead. It's in-between which is confusing. Jamie left a lot of money and a few debts. A house in the country. For a while some of his spaniels remembered him. They looked for him in the evening. Then they died too. And somehow that was the end of Jamie. Except in my heart. The house is comfortable now, and we're prosperous. But fear's the thing. Sometimes I think I only act in order to overcome my fear of acting. It isn't bad, you know, every night at 7.30 to do something you're frightened of. Even if it's only *Uncle Says No*. I think facing fear is really what it's all about, don't you, John? And that's hard to do on your own.

Blakemore It is.

Belinda How are you for friends?

Blakemore Well, I had one, a good friend, but unfortunately he decided he didn't like me any more.

Belinda His loss.

He looks at her a moment.

And family?

Blakemore You know, maybe I will have some cake.

Belinda Do. It's really good.

Belinda watches as he cuts a huge slice and puts it on a plate.

It's the best thing Christ says, I think. 'Take the hard road, not the easy one.'

Blakemore smiles and eats a large piece of cake.

Please. Keep the whole thing. I don't need it.

Blakemore I can't thank you enough. You've been wonderful.

Belinda Oh, I wouldn't say that.

Blakemore No. You have.

Belinda I know what you're thinking.

Blakemore What am I thinking?

Belinda You're sitting there thinking 'Oh God she's nice, I wish I could swap.' Boys always want each other's mothers. 'It's so annoying, I've got the wrong mother,' they think. But I promise you, in the long term, it would be even worse with me.

Duffield returns.

Duffield Well, I've been tactful for the last fifteen minutes. How are you two getting on?

Belinda Famously.

TEN

A letter from John's mother, Sheila, is projected, and at the same time heard as a voice reading.

Sheila's Voice Dear John, Not much happening here. The weather has been strange, like it can't make up its mind. Mrs Pembroke had one kidney taken out in hospital, but

45

apparently you can make do with one, which I didn't know. I tried to make apricot jam, but I haven't yet got the recipe right. It'll get better. Dad is in Fremantle, I think, I'm waiting for a letter. Short of news, I'm afraid, except to say if you never mention the *Daily Express* again, nor will we. Love, Mum.

The boys reappear and sing the hymn 'The Day Thou Gavest, Lord, is Ended'. They go.

ELEVEN

Four boys, four chairs, in the group study. Blakemore is reading his book, Sprule is playing chess on a small plastic set, Jenkins is cleaning his football boots, Gunter is on the prowl.

Jenkins I'm not going to do it.

Gunter Why? Why not? Why won't you do it? If I tell you to do something, you do it.

Jenkins Well, I won't.

Gunter I'm telling you.

Jenkins No.

Gunter Jenkins, I want you to go down to the tuck shop and get me a Coca-Cola.

Jenkins I won't go.

Gunter Then you're going to suffer horrible pain.

Jenkins Why don't you ask Blakemore?

Gunter I can't speak to Blakemore.

Jenkins Why not?

46

Gunter Because no one can speak to Blakemore. Blakemore's retreated into his shell. He doesn't talk any more. Not to people like us. He's got a new personality, haven't you, Blakemore?

Blakemore says nothing.

You see, once he'd have given us a long lecture on the nature of personality. Now we get nothing. He's got a new tactic.

Sprule Leave him alone.

Gunter He's got a new strategy!

Sprule The man is reading his book.

Gunter And suddenly he's friends with Duffield. He's discovered posh people. And rich people. He's a social climber. He adores Duffield because he's so 'refayned'. Duffield's mother gave him a fruit cake, don't ya know? And he's eating it slowly to make it last. He sits and plays pocket billiards and thinks of Belinda.

Sprule So? *So?*

Gunter looks, deciding whether to take on Sprule's unexpected challenge.

Gunter How can you play chess with yourself, Sprule?

Sprule Very easily.

Gunter Who taught you?

Sprule I saw a film with Dirk Bogarde.

Gunter And?

Sprule He plays himself at chess.

Gunter Did you know that Dirk Bogarde's tool is eighteen inches long?

Sprule Gunter, you do talk the most incredible rot.

Gunter Oh, do I really?

Sprule Yes, you do.

Gunter Well I happen to know it for a fact. It's a fact. It goes down to his knee. It creates huge problems.

Sprule I'm sure it would.

Gunter He has special trousers. Specially made.

Sprule Oh come on, Gunter.

Gunter Look at his films!

Sprule I've looked at his films.

Gunter You can see it. He has to be sewn in.

Sprule And how do you know that? How do you know that as a matter of actual factual fact?

Gunter Only, my brother happens to be best friends with the person who does it, that's all.

Sprule Your brother knows a man who sews Dirk Bogarde in?

Gunter Yes.

Sprule That's his profession? That's his job?

Gunter No, it's not his job.

Sprule Well, there you are.

Gunter His main job is driving. He's Dirk Bogarde's chauffeur.

Sprule Only every morning he has to take hold of a foot and a half of Dirk Bogarde and sew it in? I mean, does anyone ever tell you to take a flying fuck at a rolling doughnut, Gunter? And if not, why not?

Gunter No, Sprule, nobody does, because nobody has the guts.

Sprule You're just a sort of machine, aren't you, Gunter, for telling lies and making trouble? Do you have any purpose on earth except to make other people miserable?

Gunter Well, somebody has to do it, and as it happens I'm very good at it.

Sprule So you are.

Gunter (*raising his voice*) Jenkins, go down the fucking tuck shop and get me a Coke!

Jenkins No.

Sprule smiles to himself.

Sprule And perhaps you should ask yourself why your brother's best friends with Dirk Bogarde's chauffeur. Smells queer to me. What's yours, a whole family of queers?

Duffield comes in. Everyone falls silent.

Duffield So what's going on here?

Sprule Nothing, Duffield.

Gunter Have you come to speak to Blakemore? Have you come to share his cake?

Duffield I'm surprised you've got time to waste with me, Gunter. Aren't you preparing yourself for confirmation? We're all coming to chapel to see you admitted as a full member of the Church of England.

Gunter Yes, I am, Duffield. But I can't prepare without a Coca-Cola. It helps me concentrate.

Duffield Well then, why don't you go and get one?

Duffield waits.

Gunter?

Bad-temperedly, Gunter goes. Sprule and Jenkins break into applause at this victory. Blakemore goes on reading, isolated.

What was that about?

Sprule I think it's a problem for queers, don't you, Duffield? They're good at giving orders, not so good at taking them.

Duffield I wouldn't know, Sprule.

Sprule Can I ask you something, Duffield?

Duffield You can ask me anything you like.

Sprule You know what it's going to be.

Duffield I have an idea.

Duffield waits.

Go on.

Sprule Is it true?

Duffield Is what true?

Sprule Is it true you went with an air hostess in Hove?

Sprule excitedly interprets Duffield's silence as affirmative.

That's the rumour! That's what everyone's saying!

But Duffield has turned away.

Duffield Blakemore, I need a word with you.

Blakemore Of course.

Duffield Go to my study.

Blakemore To your study?

Duffield Yes. To my study.

Blakemore looks fearful.

Blakemore Right away.

Blakemore closes his book and goes out.

Duffield Sprule, you know perfectly well, a gentleman never says.

Sprule Then it is true.

Duffield You'll never know. No one will ever know. Except me and her.

Duffield goes out.

Sprule What does he want with Blakemore?

Jenkins How should I know?

Sprule I thought you were his friend.

TWELVE

Blakemore is sitting in Duffield's study with his book. Duffield takes it from him, and flicks through its pages. Silence.

Duffield It's still *L'Etranger*, is it? You're a clever fellow and you've been four weeks on the same book. Will you ever finish *L'Etranger*?

Blakemore That depends.

Duffield On what?

Blakemore Actually I've been four weeks on the same page.

Duffield You don't think fourteen is early for a mid-life crisis?

Blakemore doesn't react.

You've barely spoken for a month. You just sit and ration out Fortnum's fruit cake as if it were a sacrament. Belinda meant you to eat it, not keep it as a relic. What's happening? Have you given up?

Blakemore doesn't answer.

The Hysteric can't speak to you

Blakemore Why not?

Duffield Because he's frightened of you.

Blakemore He's frightened?

Duffield Of course. He made me do a deal. Next year's debating subjects and in return I keep an eye on you.

Blakemore frowns.

Blakemore But he's a housemaster.

Duffield So?

Blakemore It never occurred to me a master could be frightened of a boy.

Duffield Why not? Why not, Blakemore? Don't you think masters are human too?

Blakemore I don't know. It's a new thought. It's a new thought to me.

Duffield Eric feels he's failed. Don't you know that feeling? Failure?

Blakemore looks at him, cagey.

Well?

Blakemore The only thing I know, Duffield, is we shouldn't have split the atom.

Duffield Oh sure.

Blakemore That I do know.

Duffield Sure.

Blakemore As far as I'm concerned, the genie's out of the bottle and we need to put it back in as fast as possible. That's the task of my generation.

Duffield Is it really?

Blakemore Yes. Yes, it is. I don't want to look back in fifty years and say, 'I let this happen.'

Duffield You mean, you might personally end up taking the rap?

Blakemore No. No of course not.

Duffield Well?

Blakemore That's not what I'm saying.

Duffield If there's a mushroom cloud in fifty years, you think people are going to blame you? 'World War Three. This is all Blakemore's fault?' I don't think so.

Blakemore looks at him resentfully.

Blakemore Well, it doesn't matter, does it . . .

Duffield Doesn't it?

Blakemore What people think. That doesn't matter. What matters is my own conscience.

Duffield Ah, I see.

Blakemore I've got to live with myself.

Duffield Ah well, yes. We all have to live with ourselves.

Blakemore looks at him, suspicious of his tone.

Blakemore And what does that mean?

Duffield You know, Blakemore, it occurs to most of us quite early that we're going to have to slug through life in the company of someone we don't particularly like. Meaning, ourselves.

Blakemore But, Duffield, you must like yourself. Everyone else does.

Duffield Do they? Do they really?

Duffield smiles, knowing better.

And in the circumstances the only thing we can do is get on with it. Finish the book, finish the cake and move on.

Blakemore sits, chastened.

I'm leaving school in three weeks and I won't be able to help you any more.

Blakemore Where are you going?

Duffield I've decided to leave straight after my exams.

Blakemore Why?

Duffield Because I've got a round-the-world ticket.

Blakemore How did you get that?

Duffield I ran into someone in the travel business.

Blakemore Where? Where did you run into them?

Duffield Oh, you know.

Blakemore No I don't know, Duffield. Tell me.

Duffield Hove. I met her in Hove.

There is an awed silence.

Blakemore Oh God, Duffield, do you think I'll ever meet anyone in the travel business?

Duffield Yes. Your turn will come.

There's another brief silence. Then the sound of a handbell being rung down a corridor.

Voice First bell! Supper! First bell!

Duffield School means doing what you don't want to, then the rest of your life means doing what you do. The century's opening up. Think of it that way.

Blakemore I'll go to confirmation.

Duffield Do. You can always cross your fingers behind your back.

Blakemore That's what I'll do.

Duffield Try talking again. That's who you are.

Voice Second bell! Supper! Second bell!

Duffield And why not be kinder to Eric? After all, he's kind to you.

There's a longer silence, Blakemore standing, a little stunned.

Voice Third bell! Supper! Third bell!

Blakemore Thank you, Duffield.

Duffield Thank you, Blakemore.

Blakemore goes to the study door to go out.

Blakemore Good luck round the world.

MERE FACT, MERE FICTION

*A lecture delivered to the
Royal Society of Literature
in April 2010*

Last week I celebrated a melancholy anniversary. It was forty years to the day since the premiere of my first full-length play at the Hampstead Theatre Club on 6 April 1970. Those of you old enough to remember will know that the prefabricated building was moved first from one side of the Swiss Cottage car park to the other – and then back again, to somewhere nearer its original location, but now in sturdier premises. Somewhere in transit the word 'Club' dropped from the shingle. In other words, in four decades, theatre culture has changed, if not out of all recognition, at least significantly.

One further example. If you set to writing plays in the post-war years, it was necessary, or at least expected, to pass through a portal of approval. In prospect, this gave a comfortable, orderly feeling to the idea of being a British dramatist. Kenneth Tynan, a humanist dandy, guarded the portal on one side from his influential position as the *Observer*'s drama critic. Harold Hobson, a conservative Francophile whose life had been changed at the age of ten by the sight of a Bible in the illuminated window of a Christian Science church, guarded the other side from the *Sunday Times*. A novice playwright had every reason to expect that a life in the theatre would involve attracting and then retaining the interest, if not of these particular men, then at least of whoever took their place. Harold Hobson's name was inextricably linked with Beckett's and with Pinter's. Tynan's fortunes rose with his impassioned advocacy of the work of John Osborne. These were the writers they championed and whose view of the world fired them up. They were interlinked because of a profound correspondence of belief. Today, no such correspondence exists. No living theatrical figure is linked with any particular critic. Kenneth Tynan, eighty-three years old last week had he not been taken by emphysema, would be devastated to know that to work seriously in the British theatre it is no longer necessary even to know the name of the *Observer*'s theatre reviewer, let alone, God forbid, to try and read them.

Most people have an understandable nostalgia for what then felt like a common culture, even if, over the years, bitter experience left few practitioners with much trust in those delegated to be its guardians. If deference has disappeared from many areas of British life, then surely it is because many of its beneficiaries were found out to be undeserving. The growth of diversity both in the theatre audience and in the places it sharpens its opinions has brought only benefit to any dramatist whose first love is for experiment and innovation. And newspapers which once enjoyed such power find themselves discovering what it is like to live with the threat of working in a minority form.

Throughout the 1980s and beyond, militant propaganda for the free market aimed to reach out into many spheres beyond the economic. The aims of the revolution were cultural as much as political. Norman Tebbit was recently asked why the Thatcherism in which he had played such an important part had created a society he so heartily disliked. If liberating private enterprise from the shackles of the state had indeed been such an invigorating success, why were the consequences of that success so repellent to him? Lord Tebbit replied that Conservative governments of his generation had taken on such a massive task in fixing the economy that they had had no time to fix the culture. He was being too modest. In those days, there was certainly no shortage of fellow-travellers happy to direct their fire against the most communal of art forms. For years no Murdoch paper let a week go by without some loyal employee railing against their own definition of elitism – elitism usually being best represented by the state-subsidised British theatre. Why, conservative commentators asked week after week, were the routines of theatregoing so tedious? Why were the audiences so smug? Why were only a few hundred people admitted to the auditorium each night? Why were a further five thousand million excluded? Why, most of all, did plays continue to address moral and political questions which belonged more properly to the nineteenth century, and which had been definitively answered by the resurgence of an invigorated capitalism? Wasn't the form itself exhausted? Wasn't cinema hipper?

Today, such attitudes themselves look dated. Having so long prophesied The Death of the Theatre, the prophets have woken to find themselves writhing in the coils of a problem rather closer to home called The Death of the Newspaper. What a reversal of fortune! Who could have foreseen it? Research tells us that a new generation of young people from all over the country is once more choosing to go to the theatre. They seem to value its oddness, its quality of difference. Far from fearing an opportunity to concentrate, the young relish it – whereas they appear a lot less certain about needing to match their impressions of the world against opinionated sheets of paper.

If the free market is indeed the moral courtroom which its admirers claim, then what a judgement is being visited on Fleet Street. What a pack of failures the editors must be! No artistic director of a theatre could survive such a plummeting loss of income and popularity without being sacked by their board. Surely it must be, according to those iron laws of the market which newspapers have done so much to propagate, that consumers are today buying fewer newspapers because those newspapers are *poor products*. The people writing for them must be *no good* at writing. QED. Or will journalists henceforth be humbled by the decline of their own industry into less readily assuming that whatever is most popular must necessarily be most worthwhile?

The obvious absurdity of this proposition, and its roots in that same false logic which has had such currency throughout the Blair–Thatcher ascendancy, should not divert us from subtler, more interesting questions about the relationship between art and journalism, between fact and fiction. It is several of these which I aim to address tonight. When asked to name the best British film of the last twenty-five years, without thinking I nominated Adam Curtis's documentary series *The Power of Nightmares*, which examines how politicians have exploited the so-called war on terror in order to transform themselves from managers to saviours of their nation. My mind went straight to a BBC documentary rather than anything seen at my local Odeon because, clearly, *The Power of Nightmares* seemed imaginatively more ambitious than most better known fictional work. If we give Curtis's film a full body scan, the diagnosis would be that it passes some of the most traditional – if controversial – tests of art. For a start, nobody could miss the fact that it had been created by one exceptional imagination. Behind its images lay some rich associative thinking. It advanced a way of considering Western leaders which made you see familiar figures in a new light. But if you also investigated its technique, its use of what you might call scrap footage – from advertising, from feature films, from training films, as well as from more usual documentary sources – it not only adopted the methods of some of the twentieth century's most important visual artists, it also attained some of their same haunting strangeness.

You must not think that I sharpen all my aesthetic thinking by attending to Norman Tebbit, but on another occasion Tebbit showed impatience with some fellow guests in a radio studio by declaring that he was tired of hearing about the claims of art. In his view, a Rolls-Royce aeroplane engine was far more beautiful than most things living artists had created. Why was an engine not a work of art? There are certainly many different answers to his question – plenty of people would say it was – and if Tebbit's purpose were to remind us of the overlooked status of engineers then, again, many people will have sympathy. But my personal answer to the question – and please understand no one else is expected to share it – would be that an aeroplane engine is an object without metaphor, and without metaphor we have no art. An Andrew Marr television series about British history in the first half of the twentieth century is full of interesting anecdotes, one anecdote after another – here's an evacuated village, here are some servicemen dancing, here are three famous men at Yalta. But because these anecdotes refer to nothing beyond themselves, because they do not throw light on anything apart from their immediate subject, and because the images the ideas generate are pretty banal – Marr walking by the sea, Marr walking across fields, Marr in a busy street – the viewer would conclude that, whatever he or she is watching, it is not art. Marr may be a great teacher, he may be a good journalist, he is assuredly an accomplished tourist guide to what has happened and to what is known, but, by my personal definition, the one thing he cannot be is an artist.

In one provocative statement, Waldemar Januszczak, then head of arts programming at Channel 4, went even further than Norman Tebbit. He proposed that there was no need any more to make television programmes about artists because, he argued, a television programme was itself a work of art. Television had spent too long in the position of a waiter, bringing art in to the viewer on a silver salver. In the modern world, he said, television had no good reason to continue feeling subservient. Fawning profiles of artists were old hat. Television did not have to illuminate Bacon. It *was* Bacon.

Of course, such economically convenient reasoning at once blew wind-assisted through the offices of the channel controllers. Words cannot convey how delighted they were with this cute piece of postmodernism. What a rare pleasure to be let off an expensive hook by one of their own! If any idiot with a camera sounding off about anything they fancied was art, then it gave the bosses, with results we all know, an intellectually reputable excuse to drop formal arts programming more or less altogether from their majority channels. Television, it was said, now existed to be art, not to bring news of it. Strange this, because Ken Russell did not seem in the least subservient when he made his films about Delius and about Elgar. Russell seemed all too happy to accept these composers as masters, and then, in his turn, to demonstrate what their mastery had released in him. Namely, mastery.

The example of Russell making such brilliant television out of brilliant music might, you think, once and for all dispatch certain questions of category. But there is still plenty of dismaying evidence to prove how closely conjoined art and snobbery will always be. Over forty years ago Philip Roth put his finger on a problem which, in the following years, was going to challenge the novelist's profession as much as mine. He wrote that 'The actuality is continually outdoing our talents, and the culture tosses up figures daily that are the envy of any novelist.' It would be an unusual artist who did not feel that this difficulty had deepened in the new century. Having myself glibly argued for so many years that artists might more profitably look to the world around them than always to the minutiae of their own feelings for inspiration, even I have been taken aback by the sheer abundance of subject matter available in recent times. I once remarked that it was always valuable for a writer to go out and be rebuked by reality. But recently we have not been so much rebuked as overwhelmed. A working dramatist, I have found myself finishing plays about the privatisation of the railways, about the diplomatic process leading up to the invasion of Iraq, about the corruption of Labour Party funding, about Foreign Office complicity in torture and, most recently, about the financial crisis precipitated by the behaviour of the banks. But this kind of timely writing which seeks, as Balzac's work once did, to provide society with its secretarial record, continues to attract reproach from those good souls who believe that the results cannot be regarded as 'proper' plays – in the sense, say, that Sophocles or Jean Racine write 'properly'.

Particular objection – usually inarticulate – is made to the use of other people's dialogue. No sooner had a genre called verbatim drama been identified and given its vaguely lowering title than sceptics appeared arguing that it was somehow unacceptable to copy dialogue down rather than to make it up. People who did this, they said, were called journalists, not artists. But anyone who gives verbatim theatre a moment's thought – or rather, a dog's chance – will conclude that the matter is not as simple as it first looks. Nor are its moral implications. In the autumn of 2006 I was working in New York. My luck was that I could therefore go to the Lincoln Center Theater to see Jack O'Brien's superb production of Tom Stoppard's trilogy of plays, *The Coast of Utopia*. After the first evening, we were set fair. Here was the kind of epic work which wove the lives and ideas of individual nineteenth-century Russian philosophers into the overall movement of history. It was exhilarating and it was also well made. Yet at the climax of the second play the audience was jarred out of involvement. After Alexander Herzen's son Kolya was killed in a shipping accident at the age of five, Stoppard had given his father a speech in which he argued there was no need to mourn or be upset. We do not ask of a lily that it be built to last. If the child's life had indeed been brief, it was nevertheless no less perfect. 'The death of a child,'

Herzen is made to say, 'has no more meaning than the death of armies, of nations. Was the child happy while he lived? That is a proper question, the only question.'

Stoppard is self-evidently a humane and decent writer, so it would be fair to say that I came out of the production seething at his callousness. Why should he want to disfigure his work by building towards such a brutal sentiment? How could a child's life properly be compared with that of a flower? Really, this was taking the religious view of things too far. Even a priest mourns. However, when talking a few days later to a member of the production team, I was gently put right. The words were not Stoppard's. They were Herzen's. The dramatist had felt compelled to include them, against many objections, because he had wanted to give full rein to the character's unpredictability. It was a question not just of integrity but of artistic completeness. Stoppard had been taken aback that his hero, whom he so wholeheartedly admired in real life, had seemingly been so indifferent to the death of his own son. The author had included Herzen's words because they seemed to him so surprising. But nowhere in the coverage of *The Coast of Utopia* did anyone try to belittle it by labelling it as a verbatim play.

You may say that I had committed nothing more than the vulgar crime of ascribing to an author the opinions of one of his or her characters. What a crass mistake for a fellow playwright to have made! But you may also observe that the inconsistent detail, the confounding, non-fitting fact is often the giveaway mark of material drawn from life rather than the imagination. Herzen's attitude to mortality had struck us all so hard precisely because it seemed so contradictory in such a sensitive man. In James Marsh's documentary *Man on Wire*, Philippe Petit celebrates his achievement of spending forty-five minutes crossing a steel cable suspended 1,350 feet above Manhattan between the twin towers of the World Trade Centre in 1974 by coming down and sleeping with a previously unknown admirer in the street. By doing so, he instantly destroys his long-term relationship with the partner who has helped him plan his feat in the first place. Our response is to exclaim 'Oh my God, this *must* be true. It must be true because it's so unlikely.' Or maybe we use that other comforting phrase, so hated by all writers of fiction: 'Nobody could make this up.' Asked for his reasons for making the trip, Petit replied. 'When I see three oranges, I juggle. When I see two towers, I walk.' But significantly he omitted to add, 'And when I come down from two towers, I make love to the first woman I see.'

'Is this true?' 'Is this a true story?' is now the question you hear asked most frequently in cinemas. Before a film a big card regularly appears: 'This is based on a true story.' By its very blankness, the card screams authority. But all too often it also pleads immunity. It functions as a kind of prophylactic, a way of protecting the subsequent proceedings from undue criticism. By declaring in advance that something is true, the film-makers seek to absolve themselves from the highest demands of art. The implication is that if it's true, it must be interesting. And if it's ill-articulated, well then, so is life. The updated CV piously tacked on at the end of the film – telling us that the tousled hero is today running a brothel in downtown Sao Paolo, or that the loveable heroine overcame her crack habit to open a small bakery in Montecito, only later to fall victim to dengue fever, contracted with her new lover in equatorial Africa – is also intended to ward off our more spontaneous reactions to the film itself. It acts as a sort of dousing of the flame of our potential dislike.

However, this flaunting of a project's origins as proof of its worthiness seems to be more and more prevalent. Whose heart does not sink at the prospect of yet another series of half-worked television biopics – not really documentaries, not really drama – which seek to hitch a ratings ride on our foreknowledge of, say, Eric Morecambe or Tony Hancock? Who does not feel compassion for an actor who has responded to the challenge of portraying Maria Callas by getting down every one of her physical characteristics except, of course, the ability to sing demanding operatic arias better than anyone else in the world? John Maynard Keynes may have insisted that, during a recession, it was economically beneficial to set citizens to work on back-breaking, meaningless labour. They should dig holes in the road and then fill them in again. But even Keynes would stop short of asking an Equity member who was not born to dance like Nureyev to portray Nureyev. What would be the point? Is it time well spent to make a drama about Kenneth Williams in which the impersonating actor is everything but funny? Only one time in a hundred does a fictional biography like Temple Grandin's – HBO's recent compelling account of an autistic teenager whose height-ened feeling for cattle led her to design and build humane slaughterhouses all over America – not seem merely a prisoner of its own forewritten narrative. All discerning cinemagoers relish anything from Gus van Sant, but who can put their hand on their heart and say that his fiction-alised film *Milk* has anything like the resonance of Rob Epstein's documentary *The Times of Harvey Milk*, by which it is presumably inspired? Who, indeed, would go to a novelist for the most vivid and comprehensive picture of North America in the last half-century? Who would not go first to Joan Didion's essays?

'You cannot improve on the facts,' said Hilary Mantel, in a ringing defence of accuracy in historical fiction. But Mantel was most certainly not arguing that it was enough to offer only the facts. Nor is it a guarantee of importance in art that the art directs itself to an important subject. I referred at the start to Kenneth Tynan. Every Sunday, like so many other students in the 1960s, I fell out of bed and read him. But his biggest misstep surely came in the week when he reviewed Peter Watkins's film *The War Game*. Because it speculated on the effects of a nuclear attack on a typical English city, 'it might,' said Tynan, 'be the most important film ever made . . . *The War Game* stirred me at a level deeper than panic or grief . . . We are told that works of art cannot change the course of history . . . I believe this one might.' In the context of its screening, Tynan said, it was impossible to take seriously the other films released that week. An Italian director had come up with 'an ecstasy of chic self-indulgence, a gigantic parcel which conceals beneath its gaudy wrapping, a fragment of old rope'. How could anyone take seriously 'an immensely pretty film of monumental triviality' when it was placed beside a harrowing vision like *The War Game*?

Now admittedly, *Juliet of the Spirits* is not *La Dolce Vita*. But nor is it nothing. It is a film to which you may freely return many times for pleasure and instruction. And yet, oddly, in their characteristic mix of autobiography, of fiction and of fantasy, Fellini's films raise the very same question I want to ask tonight. How can there be a wrong way to make good art? And, indeed, what point does criticism serve when it asserts only 'This is not the sort of thing of which I approve?' When a tortured critic such as James Wood twists himself into a pretzel struggling to explain exactly why the particular novel he has under review is the wrong kind of good novel, then he sounds like nothing so much as a Railtrack official railing against the wrong kind of snow. All the rules dictate that, in 8½, Fellini ought not to be able to construct a counterintuitive masterpiece out of his own pampered indecisiveness. But he does.

All over the world serious work is being made in all sorts of unauthorised ways. Opinion, meanwhile, is tying its shoelaces and not noticing. In the face of the evidence, it is still held as an article of faith by high-minded observers that it takes time for artists to absorb events.

Any response that appears too quickly must, it is claimed, be journalism, not art. The fact that Wilfred Owen wrote the greatest poems of the First World War in the heat of battle does not shake the prejudice. If the high-minded had their way, Owen would have waited to lend the events more distance. He would, mind you, have been killed in the meantime, and his poems would never have got written, but at least Owen would have died with the consolation of knowing that he did at least plan to compose on a critically approved timescale. Addressing a similar conviction – that films about the occupation of Iraq and the war in Afghanistan are bound to be deeply flawed because they lack perspective – the critic David Denby asks this excellent question: 'Box-office wisdom holds that it is too early to make movies about this conflict; but how can it ever be too early to make a good film?'

It is this question of prematurity – 'Hold on, I'm not ready for this' – which bedevils the reception of any work on a contemporary subject. It is very hard in these circumstances to ensure that the question the work provokes is neither 'How soon has it been made?' nor even 'What has it been made from?' but the far more lasting question: 'How deep does it go?' I said earlier that the example for my recent plays had come from Balzac – 'What was it like living under New Labour? How did Tony Blair seem when he went to war?' But I need to make clear that I therefore regard *The Permanent Way*, *Stuff Happens*, *Murder in Samarkand*, *Gethsemane* and *The Power of Yes* as something entirely different from journalism, although they are often mistaken for it.

Journalism is reductive. This is not always the fault of journalists. It is in the nature of the job. At its best and worst, journalism aims to distil. It aims to master, even to subjugate, a particular topic. In this ambition, as every cursory reader of British newspapers will know, the journalist will always run the risk of tipping over into contempt. As soon as something can be summarised, it can also be dispatched. Anyone who has ever attended morning conference at a national newspaper will know the form: everyone taking part in the human comedy is a fool. What was once the humorous stance of *Private Eye* has become the humourless stance of the entire press. All politicians are corrupt, all manual workers are idle, all social workers are incompetent, all immigrants are scroungers. In journalism, the gap has never been wider between what people are and what they are treated as being. Only the very best journalists know how to suggest that a person, theory or event is not just what the journalist believes it to be. It is also itself. Holding that balance between your account and a proper respect for the truth of what something or somebody is *outside* your account involves a level of self-awareness hard to achieve in six hundred words.

In the West a journalistic culture which takes in both the internet and television has now become both tiring and ubiquitous. It has also led to a curious deformation in society. As citizens, we consider our family, our friends, and, most of all, our children as likeable and virtuous. But we are encouraged to consider everyone we don't know – and most especially those we know only through newspapers or holding any kind of public position – as ridiculous or vicious. To this tendency, this desire to bundle people and thereby to dismiss them, art and death are the most powerful known antidotes.

Art frequently reminds us that things are never quite as simple as they seem. Nor are people. Journalism is life with the mystery taken out. Art is life with the mystery restored. Put people on the stage, in all their humanity, propel them into a course of events, and in even the most savage satire or preposterous farce, characters may acquire a sympathy, a scale, a helplessness, all of which draw forth feelings eerily reminiscent of those elicited by people you actually know.

Meanwhile to the objection that plays and novels about contemporary events are too hastily conceived to be profound is added the confident counter-objection that such works are unlikely to endure. While William Shakespeare's plays may be crammed with incomprehensible Elizabethan references and jokes which amuse nobody, these have hardly damaged his continuing popularity. But the example of literature's highest achiever does little to blunt the popularity of this line of attack. How on earth, it is asked, can either foreign cultures or generations unborn ever be interested in such local doings? On this question, I can only say I am willing to take my chances. Like most writers, I have at best a sceptical attitude to posterity. But wherever playwrights gather, you will find them telling stories of plays, performed in far-off places and years after their premieres, which have somehow acquired what seems like an accidental shimmer.

Of a recent revival of *Stuff Happens* in Canada – six years, remember, after the National Theatre first conceived a then-topical account of the lead-up to the Iraq war – the director wrote me a letter: 'I find the play infinitely sadder than a few years ago . . . I think there is something potent about these people now officially out of office and firmly set in their historical place. At the same time, the references to both Afghanistan and Iraq are, this time, eliciting vocal responses from the audiences that I don't recall having happened in my previous production.' In response to such a letter, any playwright will argue two things. First, no proper play is ever just 'about' the events it describes. The whole intention of a play in describing one thing is to evoke another. Although *Stuff Happens* was supposedly ripped from the headlines, those who worked on its first production always rested their hopes on its allegorical resonance, its feeling for other processes and for other wars which would take it way beyond the particular path to Iraq. Bush and Blair, after all, are not the only two warmongers in history. But, secondly, in celebrating this play's bewildering success in Toronto six years on, the director was, in fact, celebrating the special nature of theatre itself. In Stalinist Russia the most powerful protest you could make was to stage *Hamlet*.

When standing as the independent candidate for the governorship of Alaska in 2006, Andrew Halcro observed of Sarah Palin that she had what any politician would kill for. 'And that is the ability to make substance irrelevant.' Theatre has the very opposite ability. It finds substance out, and weighs it with devastating accuracy. But, when deeply felt, theatre also has, like the music of Delius and Elgar, the potential to inflame the imagination of others. When *The Power of Yes* opened last October in Angus Jackson's production, it laid out the progress of the current banking crisis. It was inevitable that the immediate response be journalistic. It either was or wasn't accurate. Its diagnosis was or wasn't correct. The play suggested that bankers have come to constitute the most powerful trade union in the world, entirely dedicated to their own interests and indifferent to yours or mine. This proposition was received either with outrage or delight. The play further argued that bankers now effectively have the upper hand over anyone elected to power, firstly because complicated financial practices are sadly beyond the understanding of most democratic politicians, but secondly because bankers have refined all their various blackmail notes into one single threat, recently left like a bomb in a litter-bin: 'If you don't rig the market in our favour, we will drag you down with us.' The legitimacy of such intellectual terrorism was also hotly debated – on both sides.

Thus far, the issues raised by *The Power of Yes* might well have been batted back and forth on a lively edition of *Newsnight*. Because the play portrayed real people, and used their actual dialogue, so the dish arrived hotly spiced for journalistic carving. But then, interestingly, a second wave of reaction followed which addressed not so much the play's ideas as its techniques for deploying those ideas. Many things were expected of a play about high finance, but it was not foreseen that it should resemble Michael Bennett's production of *A Chorus Line*. Friends reported that they found the sight of twenty suited bankers lining up across the proscenium arch curiously moving. From then on, nothing was as they'd anticipated, least of all their own responses. Many spectators noticed that this was an unusual example of a verbatim play which did not seem set on righting a wrong. It did not demand the reform of the banking system, nor even, indeed, offer a rallying point for the anger against it. Verbatim theatre was, they thought, a known genre, often a touch hectoring and solemn, at its worst even self-righteous and overly dependent on direct address. On this occasion a resolute attempt was being made to jazz it, to take it places it had never been. A few smart people were clever enough to guess that the inspiration had indeed come from Glenn Gould's radio programmes, which he made over a ten-year period from 1967 onwards. In what became known as *The Solitude Trilogy*, Gould recorded the impressions of Northern Canadians, many of them living lives of extreme isolation, and then sent their voices spinning like music, weaving them, fugue-like, into something the pianist called tapestry.

The most interesting reaction of all came from a painter friend, who had seen as much as he'd listened. In particular, he had enjoyed how much the look of the play resembled an installation by Bill Viola. Short, he said, of dropping a violent cascade of water on to the actors' heads, it *was* Bill Viola. A stage language of light, form and colour had been created by the ravishing projections of Jon Driscoll, the daring of the set designer Bob Crowley, and the restless fluency of the lighting designer Paule Constable. How strange, said my painter friend, that an ostensibly prosaic, ostensibly factual play should unleash some of the purest visual poetry he had ever seen in a theatre.

It is safe to say that I was more flattered by this response than I would have been forty years previously. When I set out in the theatre, I was part of a fringe movement which often sought to crash the problem of aesthetics by doing plays as badly as possible. Or at least as crudely as possible. If you made no attempt to do things overly well, then people would not be distracted from what you were actually saying. In those days, there were brownie points only for subject matter. But, as the years went by, it became clear to me that I had not understood aesthetics at all. Aesthetics were not principally about good and bad. They were not your enemy. They were your opportunity. Style was the only means by which you could suggest that what you were writing about was something more than what you appeared to be writing about. Without style there was no suggestiveness – and with no suggestiveness, no metaphor. The processes of art could begin nowhere else.

'Are you the notorious composer Arnold Schoenberg?' someone once asked of Arnold Schoenberg. His reply has gone down in history. 'Yes. Somebody had to be.' In the last few years I admit I have felt a mild degree of fellow feeling. 'Are you the person who makes plays out of what's going on in the papers?' is never a question asked in a friendly manner. Nor is the answer much liked. 'Yes. Somebody has to.' 'How on earth do I review that?' said the theatre critic of one prominent national daily, crying out to a colleague as he left the first night of *The Power of Yes*. It is as if the doors of our theatre, of their own volition, blow shut all the time, and the task is always to prise them back open. Plenty of people get their poetry from science, from the physical universe, from the contemplation of mathematics, or of animals, or of solitude or of the stars. An audience arrives fearing the theatre to be one more medium like any other. If the subject of the play comes from political life, then they anticipate a form of animated journalism, journalism on legs, the usual mud-soup of opinion and sociology. But in fact the performing arts can deliver high-flying bankers who are at once contemptible and deeply sympathetic.

The motive behind this lecture is to point out that the word 'factual' is not synonymous with the word 'prosaic'. On the contrary. If we accept the simple distinction that factual work asks questions for us, whereas fictional work is more likely to ask questions of us, then there is no reason why some work may not do both. What matters to any artist is not where you find your materials, but where you go with them. Writing about public events may well involve an act of imagination just as profound, just as transform-ative, as for any other kind of art. And the results will be as emotionally involving. The highfalutin prejudice against any such category is misconceived. But it is only the flip side of an opposite assumption, which is equally damaging. Having recently presented to a television company a film in which at least two of the three principal characters were alcoholic, I was asked the following questions. 'What is this based on?' 'Nothing.' 'Who are these people meant to be?' 'Nobody.' 'Who are they then?' 'They're fictional.' 'Are you alcoholic yourself?' 'No.' 'Then why did you write it?' 'Because the philosophical implications of addiction are fascinating to me.' 'Do you think we should have a helpline number at the end for anyone who watches this film and is disturbed by it?' 'No.' The single fictional film has become such an endangered species on television that the automatic assumption is that it can only be a posh ver-sion of current affairs and nothing else. Nothing confuses a BBC executive more than the words 'I made it up'.

Anyone contemplating the best cinema of the twenty-first century is going to notice an extraordinary resurgence in social realism, whether in Christian Mungui's *Four Months, Three Weeks and Two Days*, in the Dardenne brothers' *L'Enfant* or in *Un Prophète* by Jacques Audiard. But although these three outstanding films – one from Romania, one from Belgium, the last from France – all deceive the audience into thinking they are watching something lifelike, underneath they are as deeply worked, as thoroughly imagined and as wholly invented as anything by Poussin or Henry James. All three boast classical plots disguised under everyday surfaces. The need for an illegal abortion, the sale of a new-born baby by his indigent father, and the rise of a young Arab criminal taking power from a Corsican gang in a French prison all provide mainsprings for stories of impoverishment in which willpower battles against fate as inexorably as in any courtly tragedy. Pontecorvo's film *The Battle of Algiers* was made in 1966, but it was projected in the Pentagon in 2003 for the benefit of officers and strategic experts then planning the occupation of Iraq. Intended to describe one situation, it blazingly illuminated another. Its portrayal of guerrilla war in Algeria in the 1950s proved relevant to another attritional fight in the following century. Fliers inviting military experts to the screening were headlined 'How to win a battle against terrorism and lose the war of ideas'. But, again, Pontecorvo had disguised his strategies as documentary.

We are living through curious times and they demand curious art – in both senses of the word. Even that most conservative of cultural critics, T. S. Eliot, confessed that you cannot contribute to a tradition unless you are determined to extend it. 'What happens when a new work of art is created is something that happens simultaneously to all the works of art that preceded it.' At the moment a handful of us are attracted to mixing fiction and reality in unfamiliar ways. *Stuff Happens* is casually referred to as a documentary play, but two-thirds of it is made up. George Bush and Tony Blair did not invite me to carry a tape recorder with them into the woods at Crawford, Texas, in April 2002, when they first conceived the momentous plan to occupy Iraq. Indeed, they did not invite anyone. There were no witnesses. To this day, nobody knows for sure what happened. So I had to invent their encounter from my imagination, pretty much as Schiller invented Mary Stuart's encounter with Elizabeth I – with the sole proviso that some version of the Blair–Bush meeting did actually occur.

'Aren't you telling us what we already know?' is the last question, always aimed between my eyes, potentially lethal in the questioner's view, but not even causing a skin wound when fired. 'No, I am not. You may think you know about something. But it's one thing to know, and another to experience.' The paradox of great factual work is that it restores wonder. Thinly imagined work takes it away. 'I never knew that, I never realised that, I never felt that' is what you hear from the departing audience when their evening has been well spent. Because we think we know, but we don't.